THE 'CELLO SOLOIST

SOLO PIECES

for

VIOLONCELLO

and

PIANO

To access audio visit:
www.halleonard.com/mylibrary

4805-3352-6487-3879

ISBN 978-1-941566-16-9

Exclusively Distributed By
HAL•LEONARD®
7777 W. Bluemound Rd. P.O. Box 13819 Milwaukee, WI 53213

Visit Hal Leonard Online at
www.halleonard.com

Over thirty years ago in Switzerland my father, an amateur musician who had a complete collection of Music Minus One recordings then available for a number of instruments (at different times he had played the piano, violin, viola and bassoon), gave me my first LP of the piano accompaniment to a set of pieces titled *Solos for the 'Cello Player.* Over the next few years I had countless hours of fun and frustration playing along with my record, gradually learning to play all the pieces. Some were relatively straightforward, technically, and some seemed so difficult that at first, I could not even imagine what they were supposed to sound like.

No one at the time could have imagined that, more than thirty years later, I would be enjoying a rich, rewarding life as a professional cellist, even less that MMO would approach me to re-record those same works over the very same piano part, recorded before I was born, which had been my invisible partner for so long.

This new MMO issue includes complete versions of seventeen wonderful treasures, and I believe that with this reference, the frustration I felt years ago will be minimized or even eliminated for players of all levels.

The works on this recording are organized so that a complete play-through is palatable, yet are divided into groups so that studying a smaller number of pieces can be a very satisfying project. These groups are stylistically and tonally coherent and provide contrasting Tempi. The first four pieces make up a less-difficult Baroque set (I consider the Marie *Cinquantaine* to be in the Baroque style). The next four are a harder Baroque group. The Beethoven to Schumann works comprise the Classical-Romantic set, and the final four pieces are Late-Romantic/Early Impressionistic (well, perhaps this stretches the labels a bit, but I am sure you will find they do have a lot in common!). Except for the Baroque sets, I have avoided making choices based on the estimated difficulty of the works, simply because we all find different aspects of 'cello-playing difficult. Depending on individual techniques and musical sensibilities, for example, one will find the Popper very challenging, while another will be tested by the perfection of Brahms' Lullaby. I myself have always found *The Swan* to be a greater test of my nerves in concert than, say, the Dvorák *Concerto....* Certainly, 'cellists of all levels will find works that are accessible within each stylistic group.

If these great works provide you with half the fun and inspiration I had thirty years ago and while revisiting them for this recording, we will have succeeded. And who knows, perhaps MMO will be calling you in thirty years!

- Steven Thomas

Music Minus One

3726

CONTENTS

Pergolesi: *Tre Giorni*: Nina. 7
Gabriel Marie: *La Cinquantaine* 8
Gluck: *Orfeo*: Andante 9
J.S. Bach: Suite No 3, BWV1009: *Bourrées I and II* 10
Antonio Lotti: Aria 11
Jean Baptiste Senaillé: Allegro Spirituoso *(from Violin Sonata in D minor)*. 12
Händel: Larghetto *(from Violin Sonata, op. 1, no. 13)* 14
Händel: Allegro *(from Violin Sonata, op. 1, no. 15)* 14
Beethoven: Andante *(arranged from the 'Andante Favori' for piano, WoO57)*. 16
Mozart: Divertimento, KV334: Menuet 18
Brahms: Lullaby 19
Weber: Country Dance 20
Schumann: 5 Pieces in Folk Style: Lento 21
Debussy: Romance 22
Saint-Saëns:
Carnaval des Animaux: La Cygne (Carnival of the Animals: The Swan) ...23
Fauré: *Sicilienne* 24
Popper: Village Song, op. 62, no. 2 26
Tuning Notes: A440

NOTES ON THE WORKS

BAROQUE SET I

PERGOLESI — This simple, charming piece can readily be attempted by anyone, since it can be played almost entirely in first and fourth positions. Occasional shifts into third position are straightforward enough that I have often given this to students who had not yet been introduced to this position. With a very manageable tempo, technical considerations will not interfere with the much more satisfying pursuit of beautiful sound and dynamic contrast.

MARIE — Only marginally more demanding than the Pergolesi, this too can be played mostly in first and fourth positions plus the "a" harmonic. Because of the amount of repetition within the tune, the length of this piece should not daunt beginners–there are relatively few notes to learn, and once again, one can concentrate on the things that really matter, such as style and finding an endless variety of ways to play repeated melodies.

GLUCK — Even if you have not studied past the fourth position, do not shy away from this piece. Its beauty and familiarity make it an ideal way to start exploring those higher notes! And if you are not yet comfortable with tenor clef, this piece will introduce you to it nicely. And for you more advanced players, you have probably already figured out that it is harder to play this with the requisite purity of sound than you first thought!

BACH — If this is your introduction to Bach, may this be the beginning of your most rewarding, life-long musical journey. This movement can be played almost entirely in first position (it most probably was in Bach's day), and any other fingering is just additional refinement. The piano accompaniment (not Bach's original intention) should help underline one of the most inspiring aspects of his solo suites: *implied* harmony.

BAROQUE SET II

LOTTI — Less-advanced players should not overestimate the difficulty of this piece. The bowings and fingerings I have provided are somewhat of an ideal, and if they seem overly challenging at first, I would recommend using more separate bows with downbows on the downbeats and retreating to the safety of first and fourth positions wherever possible–the music will still sound beautiful! Be aware also that in the baroque style, long notes tend to be released, and during these releases there is always time to move around the fingerboard with no hurry.

SENAILLÉ — This work is fast and difficult, but definitely playable. Even if the second half seems too hard at first, it is worth playing the slightly less demanding first page just to get into the spirit of the music, and I am certain that that will provide the inspiration for putting in the extra practice to learn the second page. You may consider playing measures 39-72 down an octave to make them more accessible. Since this movement is transcribed from a violin sonata anyway, changing the register does not adversely affect the music.

HÄNDEL (Larghetto) — I have taken the liberty of re-writing the rhythm of the original (dotted-quarter-eighth at the beginning of the first measure and subsequent similar ones) to match authentic performance practice. This is a great piece for confidently exploring the first six positions since most of the shifts are small and occur during released long notes.

HÄNDEL (Allegro) — This is the toughest piece so far, jumping all over the fingerboard and with some challenging thumb position work. I strongly recommend slow, methodical practice taking care to be consistent with fingerings. Gradually speed up (using a metronome for this is really helpful) and eventually, it *does* become less difficult!

CLASSICAL/EARLY ROMANTIC SET

BEETHOVEN — Most of this arrangement is not difficult once you have figured out the rhythms, so attention can be given to finding different ways of playing the many repetitions of the melody. One should not be bound to the printed dynamics here (though it is best not to make a habit of this!), most of which are just my own suggestions. The last phrase is indeed difficult, but if approached with confidence in the left hand, even those with no experience reaching that high can play it. Simply keep playing *forte* with the left hand while making the diminuendo with the bow.

MOZART — Mozart's music seems so difficult to play well because we want it to sound pure, simple and innocent, yet full of richness and depth. If we respect it without fear, and realize he always wrote in a way that gave the performer time to express and the listener time to com-prehend, it is no longer so daunting.

BRAHMS — This Lullaby seems too short, but perhaps that is why it is so perfect. Unfortunately this piece has become almost too familiar, and one will find it easy at first. As one immerses oneself in it, however, it becomes increasingly beautiful, and subsequently more and more difficult.

WEBER — The treble clef notwithstanding, this typically lighthearted Weber work is not too difficult. For those not familiar with thumb position this is a fun and easy way to begin: just place your straightened left thumb perpendicularly across the fingerboard on the "a" and "d" harmonics where indicated - you don't even need to press down, just touch the strings.

SCHUMANN — Finding personalized fingerings is the secret to playing this piece, so time spent experiment-ing will be well spent. It is virtually impossible to play this with all the smoothness that Schumann wrote and clearly intended. However, even as notes are released to allow for string crossings or shifts, if the bow keeps moving and the left hand makes smooth, unhurried connections, an illusion of complete *legato* will be main-tained.

LATE ROMANTIC/IMPRESSIONIST SET

DEBUSSY — There are no special secrets to playing this most "intangible" music. It is all about tone color. Just about any fingering or bowing is good, so long as it enables you to pursue your ideal sound at any given moment.

SAINT-SAËNS — This, more than any other piece in our repertoire, is associated with the 'cello in everyone's mind (possibly more so than even a Swan!). I find that the image of a swan's effortless motion helps in one's physical approach to this work, just as the picture of the swan's sharply-defined, strong yet graceful neck inspires us to produce a focused, quietly confident and always warm sound.

FAURÉ — More than any other piece on this recording, this lives by the interplay between piano and cello. Once you can let yourself be carried by the wonderfully played lilt in the piano part, the notes will almost play themselves. This is another work that may seem long, but because of the amount of repetition in the melodies, it can be learned fairly quickly. I would recommend listening to the recording of the piano part alone while *imagining* the 'cello part before attempting to play it.

POPPER — Not only was Popper the composer/performer who gave most to the development of our instrument, he is a greatly underrated composer. Yes, this is a difficult piece, but because Popper knew the instrument so well, he managed to write things that seem more difficult (therefore brilliant) than they really are. The big upward swoops are all to harmonics, downward big shifts are to comfortable positions, and thumb position material is limited and basic. If the double-stops don't work at first, the top-line alone will sound adequate. We have taken a conservative tempo to allow even intermediate players to attempt this piece without missing out on any of its incredible charm. (A word about measure 41: the original music had a *fermata*, as shown, but for practicality, on the recording we have simply added one beat (shown as a rest above the staff, though there would be nothing wrong with holding the note for that extra beat).

—Steven Thomas

EDITOR'S NOTE ON THE TEXT

IN REEDITING ALL THE MUSIC IN THIS COLLECTION I have taken the liberty of changing some bowings from the original arrangements for a variety of reasons (practicality, *Urtext* editions, contemporary research on authenticity). Fingerings are provided, but I hope that this will only stimulate the search for even better, individually suited ones, and for variety on repeats. I have occasionally altered the original to facilitate playing with the recording (for example, there should be a *fermata* in measure 28 of *Nina*, but to fit it with the accompaniment, it is easier to read it as printed in this book).

—*Steven Thomas*

Nina

G. B. Pergolesi
(1710-1736)

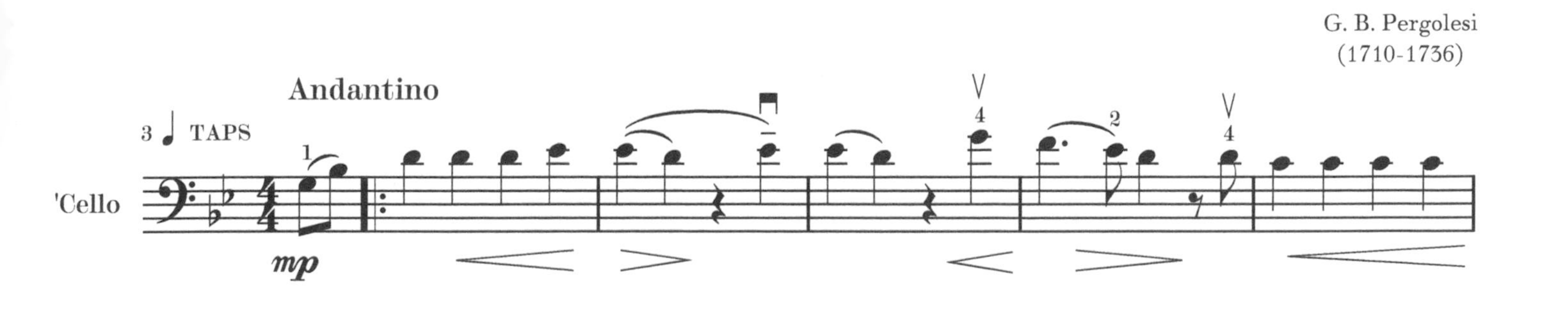

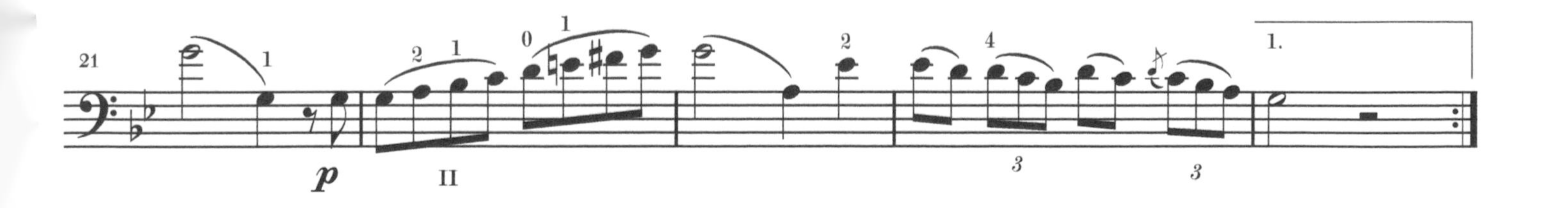

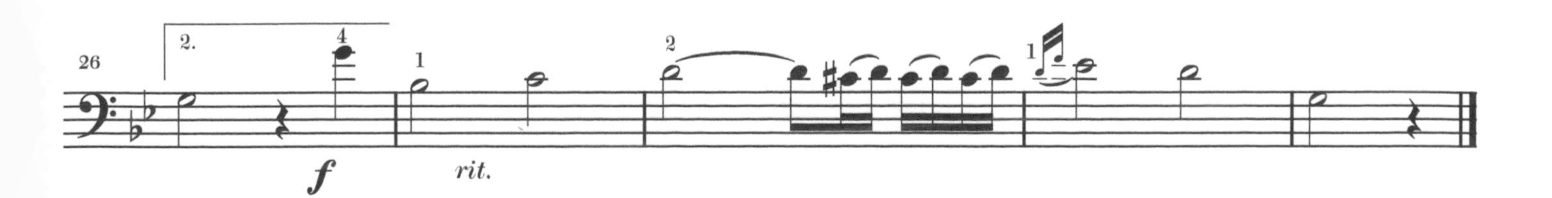

La Cinquantaine

Gabriel Marie
(1852-1928)

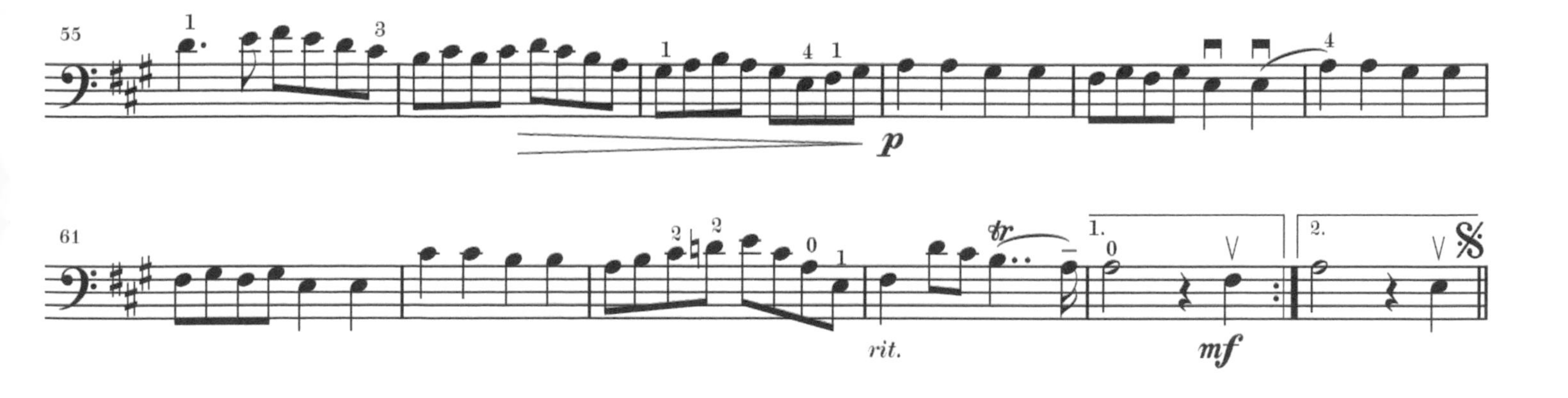

Andante

from **Orfeo**

C. W. von Gluck (1714-1787)

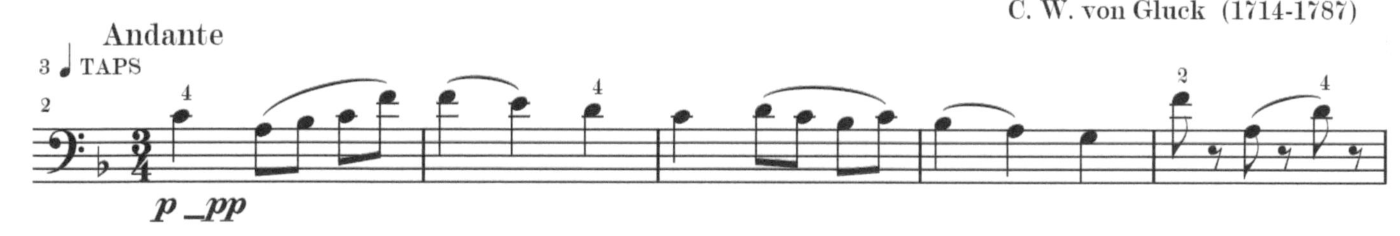

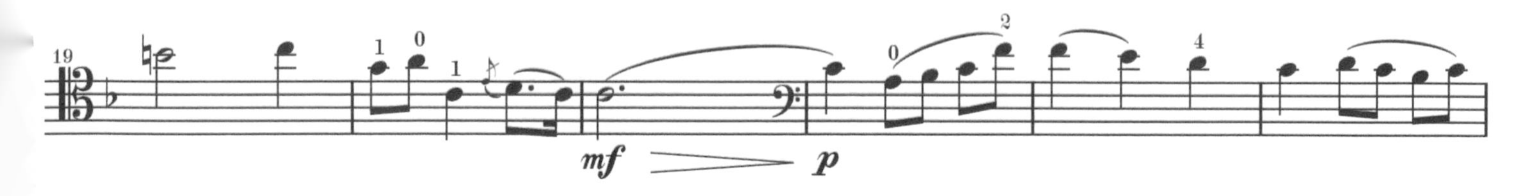

from Suite No. 3, BWV1009

Aria

Antonio Lotti
(1667-1740)
Allegretto grazioso
'Cello
mf
pp
poco rit.
D.S. al Fine
Fine

Allegro Spirituoso

from Violin Sonata in D minor

Jean Baptiste Senaillé
(1687-1730)

cresc.

cresc.

meno mosso
a tempo

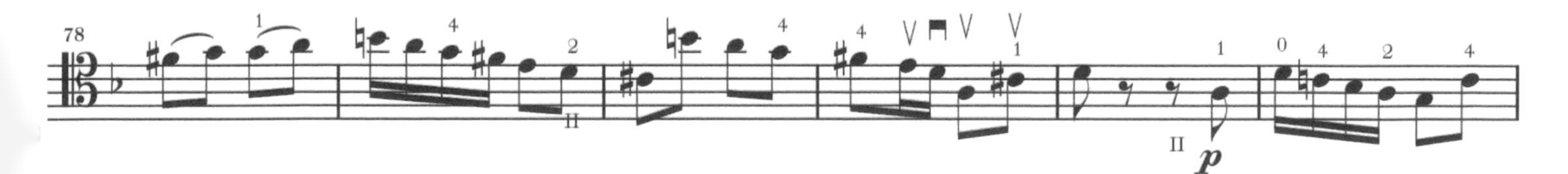

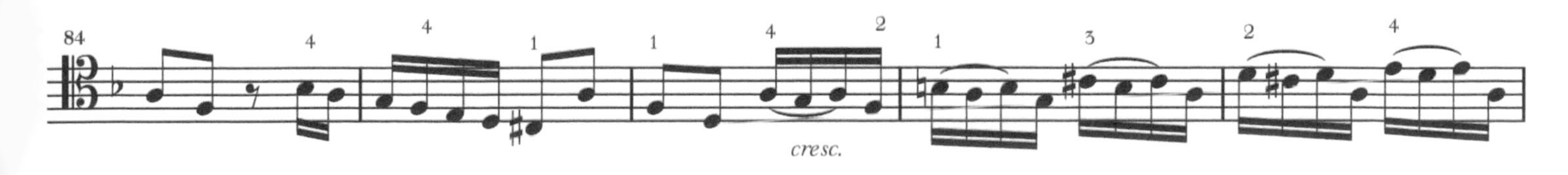
cresc.

cresc.

Larghetto

from Violin Sonata, op. 1, no. 13

G.F. Händel
(1685-1759)

Allegro

from Violin Sonata, op. 1, no. 15

G.F. Händel
(1685-1759)

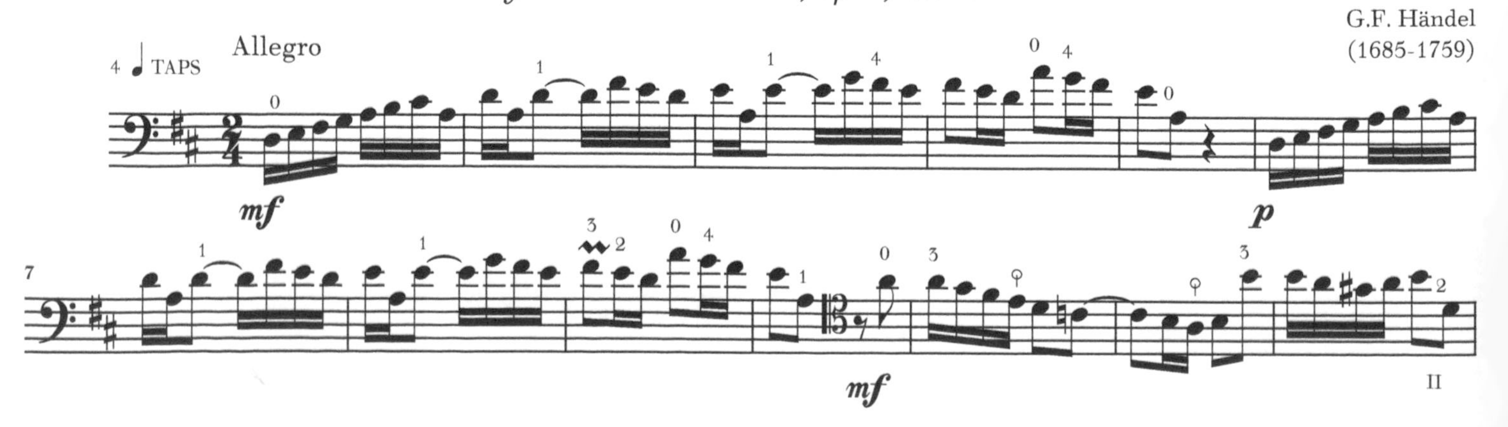

14
p
cresc. poco a poco
mf

19
p cresc.
f

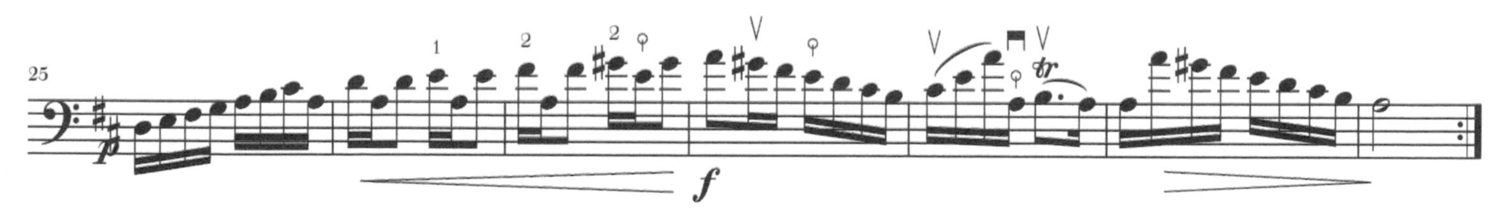
25
p
f

32
p
II
mf

38
p
I
mf
f

44
p

50
mf
p
cresc. poco a poco

55

61
f

Andante

Arranged from the 'Andante Favori' for piano, WoO57

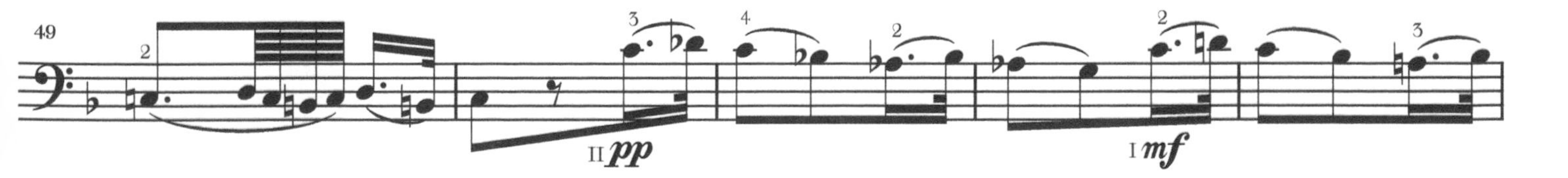

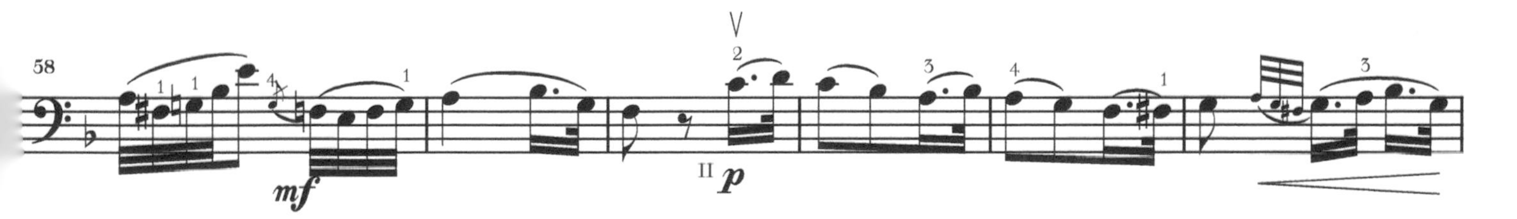

cresc. poco a poco

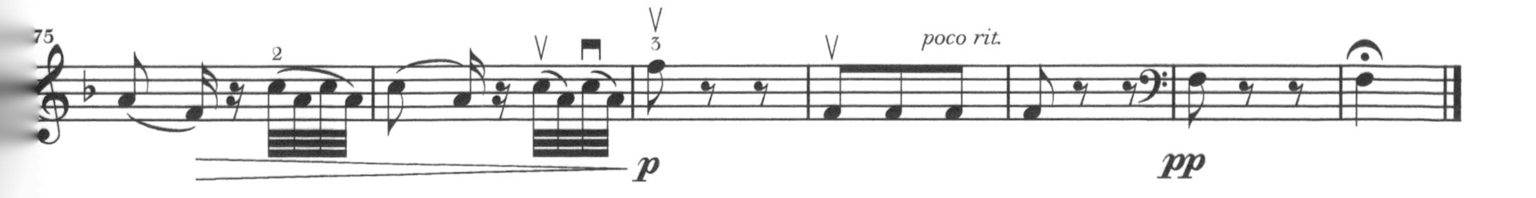
poco rit.

Menuet

from Divertimento, KV334

Wolfgang Amadeus Mozart
(1756-1791)

46
49
mf
cresc.
54
mf
p

58
cresc.
f
D.C. al Fine

Lullaby

Johannes Brahms
(1833-1897)
Andante
TAPS
pp
mp
pp
II
rit.

Country Dance

Carl Maria von Weber
(1786-1826)

Lento

from 5 Pieces in Folk Style

Robert Schumann
(1810-1856)

Romance

Claude Debussy
(1862-1918)

La Cygne (The Swan)

from Carnaval des Animaux (Carnival of the Animals)

C. SAINT-SAËNS (1835-1921)

Sicilienne

Gabriel Fauré
(1830-1914)

39
p

44
pp
II
dolce
II

50
III

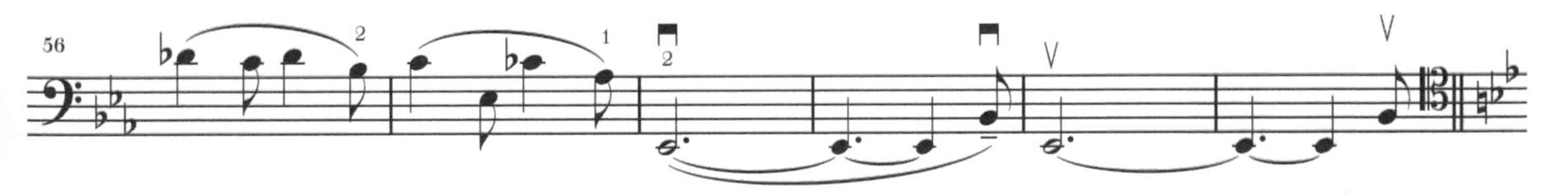
56

62
f
p
f

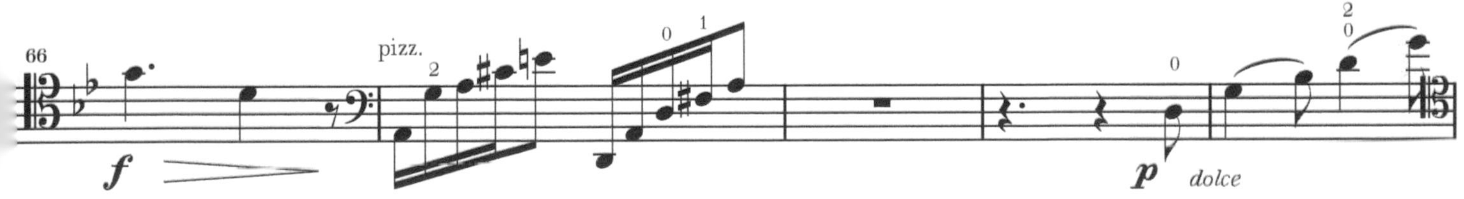
66
pizz.
f
p
dolce

71

76
pp

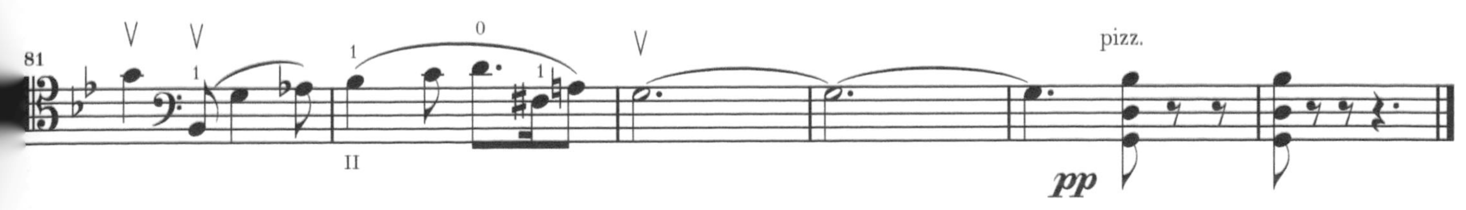
81
II
pizz.
pp

Village Song

David Popper
(1846-1913)

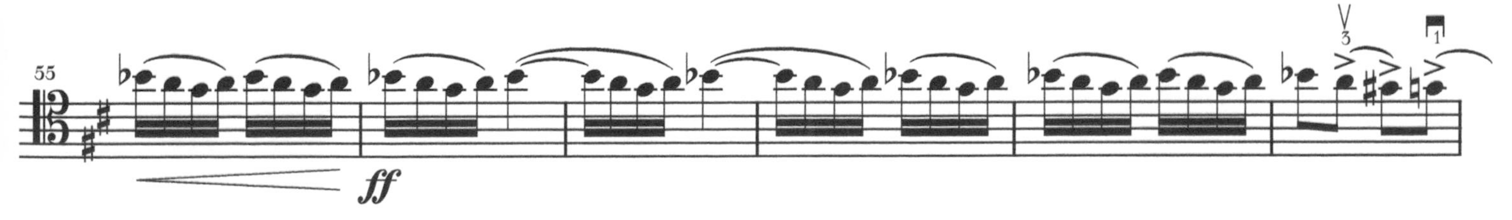
55
ff

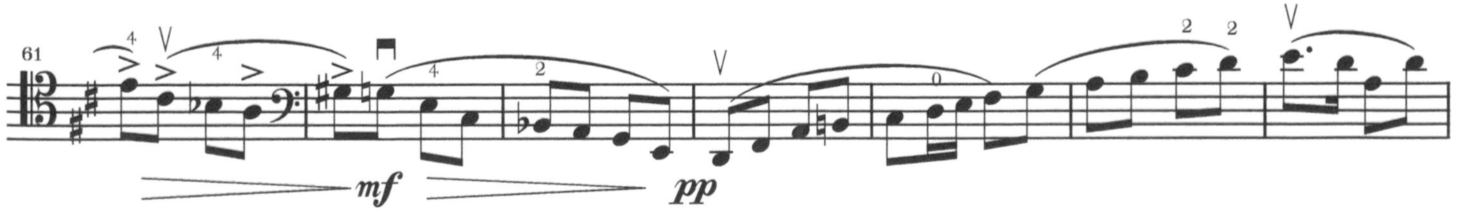
61
mf
pp

68
p

75

87
mf

94
p

101
mp
mf
f

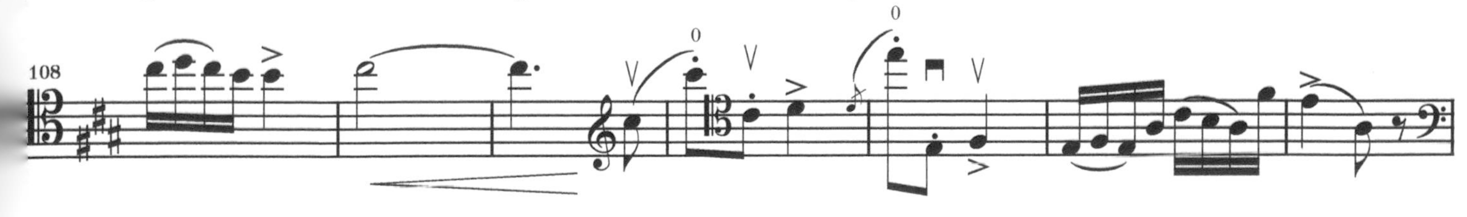
108

115
p
pizz.
f
p

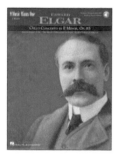

e Hal Leonard Classical ıy-Along™ series will help ı play great classical pieces. ten to the full performance cks to hear how the piece sounds h an orchestra, and then play ng using the accompaniment cks. The audio CD is playable any CD player. For PC and Mac ıputer users, the CD is enhanced you can adjust the recording to tempo without changing pitch.

OZART:
UTE CONCERTO IN D MAJOR, K314
CD Pack
341 Flute....................$12.99

AMMARTINI:
ESCANT (SOPRANO) RECORDER ONCERTO IN F MAJOR
CD Pack
342 Soprano Recorder....................$12.99

EILLET:
EBLE (ALTO) RECORDER NATA IN G MAJOR, OP.1, NO.3
D Pack
343 Alto Recorder....................$12.99

ZART:
ARINET CONCERTO IN A MAJOR, K622
D Pack
344 Clarinet....................$12.99

ZART:
RN CONCERTO IN D MAJOR, K412/514
D Pack
346 Horn....................$12.99

CH:
LIN CONCERTO IN A MINOR, BWV 1041
D Pack
347 Violin....................$12.99

EMANN:
LA CONCERTO IN G MAJOR, TWV 51:G9
line Audio
48 Viola....................$12.99

9. HAYDN:
CELLO CONCERTO IN C MAJOR, HOB. VIIB: 1
Book/CD Pack
00842349 Cello....................$12.99

10. BACH:
PIANO CONCERTO IN F MINOR, BWV 1056
Book/CD Pack
00842350 Piano....................$12.99

11. PERGOLESI:
FLUTE CONCERTO IN G MAJOR
Book/CD Pack
00842351 Flute....................$12.99

12. BARRE:
DESCANT (SOPRANO) RECORDER SUITE NO. 9 "DEUXIEME LIVRE" G MAJOR
Book/Online Audio
00842352 Soprano Recorder....................$12.99

14. VON WEBER:
CLARINET CONCERTO NO. 1 IN F MINOR, OP. 73
Book/CD Pack
00842354 Clarinet....................$12.99

15. MOZART:
VIOLIN CONCERTO IN G MAJOR, K216
Book/CD Pack
00842355 Violin....................$12.99

16. BOCCHERINI:
CELLO CONCERTO IN B-FLAT MAJOR, G482
Book/CD Pack
00842356 Cello....................$12.99

17. MOZART:
PIANO CONCERTO IN C MAJOR, K467
Book/CD Pack
00842357 Piano....................$12.99

18. BACH:
FLUTE SONATA IN E-FLAT MAJOR, BWV 1031
Book/CD Pack
00842450 Flute....................$12.99

19. BRAHMS:
CLARINET SONATA IN F MINOR, OP. 120, NO. 1
Book/CD Pack
00842451 Clarinet....................$12.99

20. BEETHOVEN:
TWO ROMANCES FOR VIOLIN, OP. 40 IN G & OP. 50 IN F
Book/CD Pack
00842452 Violin....................$12.99

21. MOZART:
PIANO CONCERTO IN D MINOR, K466
Book/CD Pack
00842453 Piano....................$12.99

HAL•LEONARD®

Prices, content, and availability subject to change without notice.

www.halleonard.com